TO EVERY THING
A SEASON

Books by Joyce Hifler

TO EVERY THING A SEASON

THINK ON THESE THINGS

TO EVERY THING
A SEASON

Joyce Hifler

Illustrations by Ray Cruz

DOUBLEDAY & COMPANY, INC.   GARDEN CITY, NEW YORK
1969

The author wishes to acknowledge with
appreciation the World Publishing Company and Executive Editor Sid Steen for
use of material which originally appeared
in her column in the Tulsa *Daily World*.

Contents

Contents

"To every thing there is a season, and a time to every purpose under heaven. . . ."

Ecclesiastes 3:1

DEDICATED TO MY DAUGHTER, JANE
AND TO
MY MOTHER, NELLIE SEQUICHIE

Life has its seasons . . . fresh, young, unpredictable . . . fretful at times . . . and yes, golden and strong in labor . . . rapid in growth . . . brave and pensive and fruitful . . . blending gradually until . . . one season is well on its way . . . before another has quite finished its work. . . .

Through all seasons . . . through all the swift changes . . . of cold and heat . . . emotional outbursts . . . strengths and weaknesses . . . the pendulum of preservation swings wide with faith . . . because man can still control . . . the changes in his life . . . so that a springlike atmosphere . . . prevails right through autumn and winter . . . however hard the conditions seem . . . outside himself . . . if he has . . . an inner strength . . . he has nothing to fear . . . for then he knows. . . . He knows the changes are beautiful . . . beautiful in their very nature . . . created to be so. . . . And man need not resist . . . nor cry, nor find war a necessity . . . for there is a time in every life . . . a time to be born . . . a time to laugh . . . a time to weep . . . a time to seek . . . a time to love . . . a time to keep silence . . . a time for every purpose . . . a purpose for every thing under heaven!

Chapter 1

"A time to be born, and a time to die. . . ."

I've shared with you some happy things I thought would never die. . . . I gave my heart without the thought you'd ever make it cry. . . . I thought with time the things we'd share . . . would never pass away. . . . I thought the tenderness of love was forever and a day. . . . I thought my God had touched your heart and spirit, dear and kind . . . would never let me lonely be or hurt I'd ever find. . . . I thought, or did I think, as I blindly walk the way . . . the lonely often know so well . . . they walked it yesterday.

Spring went to bed last night in tears. While rain dripped from the eaves, sleep came drifting, dreaming, a thankful sort of experience to warm and relax the body and mind, to make easier those things of positive light, and to know that all things are in God's hands.

Spring awoke this morning with geese winging their way northward and blue smoke lying close to the earth under pressure from her temper. She will feel better right away, because in the distance there are patches of bright green and a new dress in the making. Soon there will be blossoms, sweet and fragrant, to nest the bluebirds and a new birth will burst over the earth with the freshness of jonquils and the color of heaven.

There is something about the deep woods in any season that inspires man to live now, but in spring when all that sleeps awakens the very atmosphere is life! Here the sunlight sifts through heavy foliage, coloring the very air with the shade of new leaves. Beneath the fern fronds in a soft, dry, little nest of last year's leaves are baby rabbits cuddled in furry comfort. A squirrel chatters first at the blue jay and then to warn any intruder to keep its distance.

The activity of nature is felt long before it is visible.

Footsteps must fall softly and easily, and form and movement must learn to blend before they gain acceptance here. There is a natural telepathy that silently alerts the whole forest to an outsider. Frequently, the only sound is the tiny waterfall gurgling and splashing just after a spring shower. Violets, deep purple and lush, nest in rich green leaves along the banks of the stream. May apples overshadow smaller woods plants to protect tiny blue flowers. Gnarled grapevine, as old as time, twists black and tangles among new growth. And if one takes on the new birth, maintains an emotional calmness, a sense of deep spiritual agelessness, allows all the distrust, fear, hurt, and infirmities of the race to die away, he can become a part of the deep woods in spring. He will know he has gained acceptance by a chorus of a hundred different voices and sounds that mingle together in the flowering plum as it shimmers white and breathlessly beautiful along the slope. Here is creation. Here is a time to be born.

※

Morning begins in the dark. The merest suggestion of light sifts among the stars washing away their glitter and paling the moon. But night clings rapaciously, always darkest just before it is nudged away by the soft rose tints of dawn.

Maturing slowly, morning allows earth's creatures a little more rest, a bit more time to adjust to a different pace. Once awakened it is riotous with activity and filled with energy and bustle.

A spring morning can penetrate the darkest soul and sweep out every unhappy thought because it comes equipped with a birthday. The old one ended last evening when something no longer needed was left behind. It is a new day, a challenge to change. And man has a right to a new birth, a right to claim his inheritance from that which is infinitely greater than all the family trees. It is his Divine Birthright. He no

4

longer needs to be burdened with who he is or who he is not. He no longer must live with continual fear because of what he has heard or by a tangle of superstitions. They have no place in his new life and he can now seek out Truth for himself.

We were not born to die but to live! And to live more abundantly! A season to every purpose under heaven! And this is the morning of newness, a time when all of life sweeps wide a blaze of new hope!

*

Like so many beginners, spring often has a bit of harshness to it. It has not yet learned that everything will respond to it better when it speaks in honeyed tones. And just as the great discovery is made, it loses its temper again and shuts out all the warmth of nature's love. And so typical of the old, all nature looks with adoring eyes upon spring's youthful, capricious acts and tries and tries again for that hint of mellowness that promises growth. It so often happens that its wild behavior closes doors, and disapproving sounds admonish that when it can behave as befitting a livable season it can come in. And suddenly it has the smooth, smiling face of a child, glowing warm and bubbling with vitality. It wears flowers in its hair and has a breath of mellow warmth. Its song is the voice of the robin and the whistle of the redbird. No one could resist its fragrant nights and breath-taking mornings when such freshness settles gently on Mother Earth like a misty, glittering veil through the lush green.

Then, in a wild torrent of tears it fills to overflowing the wrinkles on the face of Mother Earth. It varies between its tempestuous ways, which makes all that love it cower, and the gentleness, which invites everything to come closer and love it more. So old and yet so young in heart it sets the scene

5

for procreation. Whether it is a flurry of wings, pollen in a wild mixture, or the touch of human fingers, all of God's creation feels the pull of newness. Old as the first creation, it remains refreshingly new and wildly exciting, always knowing that this must be the first time, untouched, untamed, unbelievably beautiful. A time to be born, forgetting there was ever another birth, because this is the important one— the important time—NOW!

*

Would God take a human being so marvelously made and in such a brief span of life have his journey completed? Or is this one more phase in man's development, one more lap on the journey to a perfect soul? Am I the same spirit, the same One, the whole of one person as I started out to be? Or am I bits and pieces of greater souls, maybe some of lesser, yet as the pieces fit into place, ruled by the best or the strongest or most dominant, no matter what it might be. I cannot believe I was born knowing nothing, free of past hindrances, inherent except by thought—dwelling on what my eyes and heart conceive. I cannot believe I am limited to this brief time, but that I am here to work and to carry with me knowledge to do a greater work. How can we be like the lazy old sun, lying around heaven all day? But the Universe with its creativity, its generously endowed possibilities, holds a tremendous interest. It is that creativity which holds the stars in their course and the world's part in the pattern of things.

What of the pianist's talent to play, by natural ear, music he has never heard before? What helps the sculptor carve the perfect face—the artist paint the perfect scene? Without training, who gave these powers to the artist?

When I am amazed at the distance I have come, seemingly alone and without much to guide me—where did I begin?

6

Was it before I was visible? When my own mother carried me, was there a soul born too, or was there a spirit sent by God to be housed in this body, this temple? Outside myself, why do we think this world is alone in the Universe? Does God not have the ability to create other worlds and are they not inhabited with possibly more developed souls than this one—or less? When we go beyond this world, do we die or do we graduate?

Have we not seen conditions change when we pray? Is He a faraway somebody that hears us sometimes or is He the Ever-Present, All-Wise Master that sees our every move, knows our every need, rejoices when we follow through as we should? And when we drop beneath His Holy eyes, does He not hear our cry and lift us up again?

Let me not be so limited in my thinking that I fail to use the wisdom given me to develop quickly, to believe deeply, to know life for its real reason—to see good—and not evil.

✳

The natural processes of the coming and going of the physical man remain something of a miracle and more of a mystery. But there is nothing miraculous or mysterious in the ways of those who have breath but do not live. How common the thought that to be alive is immoral.

Man chooses where he shall give up, where he shall die, and it may be in his daily routine. Following along in a familiar rut day after day, seeing but not feeling; trying but not caring; thinking but not deeply; loving, but so remotely; and turning aside from everything that would suggest new ways or new thought. This is being one of the old skins that could never hold new wine. Is he dying while he is waiting to live?

His routine is a simple one, as prompt and trustworthy

8

and monotonous as the clock itself. Arising every morning not one dot before or after the appointed hour. The routine is so polished and so executed that one thing out of place can throw the whole cycle. But on it goes day after day, the same job at the same desk among the same people waiting to hear the same bell to tell them to eat the same kind of lunch while talking about the same things and so it goes. Unless, of course, something scandalous happens to whisper about and to secretly shake secure routines, something too close for comfort.

Man's inflexible routine resembles something without life until by accident or by a drastic change, a bit of life and sparkle filter in and it is like having risen from the dead to find something new has been added to the world in the name of joy. It is life, the very ingredient that rigid routine forgets exists in its lifeless comfort.

"Awake, O Sleeper, and arise from the dead!" is a strange cry to a person who believes himself only comfortable. And if he is ever awakened he can no longer be happy as a sleeper. If he so chooses, one day he will run a finger down the list of requirements for living and find: willingness to change, cheerfulness, awareness of life, compassion, generosity, and faithfulness.

Life is sharing, but living is having something to share as an individual, as one who has stepped out of the gray area and can see and taste and feel life as something not routine and automatic, but rich and gracious and good and marvelous. Life is NOW!

Chapter 2

"A time to plant, and a time to pluck up that which is planted. . . ."

I have a garden in my mind . . . in which I walk sometimes . . . and in the glowing gold . . . of a setting sun . . . a rose of courage climbs . . . and finds its way along the fence . . . that protects and holds my heart. . . . And all along the walk of love . . . the flower of peace makes its start. . . . A mockingbird in all its joy . . . sings deep within the night. . . . And rest comes gently drifting down . . . and settles oh so lightly . . . upon my grateful heart serene . . . and I spend my tranquil hours . . . within the garden of my mind . . . among the fragrant flowers.

When the air becomes particularly soft and sweet, though rain and sleet have left a field of diamonds and pearls glittering and bejeweling the fields about, then it is nearing a time to plant. The heart of the productive world is stirred long before the sap begins to run. Wintry fingers are still tapping on frosty windows when life knocks loudly on the door and invites a new world of wonder to come out and be seen. Crocus and grape hyacinths bloom bright gold and purple in the snow, and fingers of green poke their way with sheer bravado through a still-crusty earth. The tide of the year changes and suddenly—as though a thousand unseen sopranos break the silence—there is a time to plant!

"I have planted, Apollos watered; but God gave the increase. So then neither he that planteth anything, neither he that watereth; but God that giveth the increase. Now he that planteth and he that watereth are one: and every man shall receive his own reward according to his own labor."

It is sad when we try to reap and realize we have not planted. Whether it is a garden of flowers, a garden of compassion, love, joy, or well-being, the sowing must precede the reaping. And even then we must do and bless our work, for God is at the source of that which we accomplish.

We must always plant brave gardens with vivid colors of

the red rose, the gold of the marigolds, the lavender and purple of the fragrant lilacs. In our efforts to plant well, we are often astonished that such richness unfolds. From year to year we forget what we have planted and the beauty reseeds and comes again in a new radiance to cheer the heart. After a time we come to expect the little forgotten happinesses that multiply and surprise us when we most need them. But we must not forget the importance of the first planting.

There is yet another brave garden to plant. This is the garden in the heart. We must be sure never to plant a weed, for love will not grow where weeds choke it. Anger and fear planted in the heart will leave no room for the things that comfort. There are garden paths along which we walk daily that become overgrown with thorns and vines that make us stumble. In allowing them to take root and grow, they soon cripple us. Then there is no longer a garden where there is beauty, but only a weed patch where trouble grows.

There must be discipline in our planting, for allowing vagrant seeds to take root in the garden of the heart may produce a fruit that is intensely sweet, but small and tart to burn the tongue. It can end in bitterness. Cultivation of one's garden is all important and will give a life that is full and sweet and satisfying, but we must never tarry when there is other planting to do. There is a time to pluck that which is planted. When we wait too long, the fruit loses its flavor and decays.

We can plant, Apollos waters, but God gives the increase and the wisdom to know when to plant and when to pluck that which is planted.

*

Sometimes we reap only experience in our efforts toward excellence. Yet, we must not hesitate for lack of heart to tackle something simply because we do not believe the returns are great enough. How can we know what abundance we may reap if we invest the best efforts, plant the best seeds, and expect the best life has to offer.

The forces of life have a way of fitting things together in a successful pattern we alone would never have the intelligence to conceive. Even when there are unpleasant experiences we can find within them an opportunity to rise above ourselves and perhaps a step higher in human understanding. We can reap something from every experience if we choose to be taught and not just complain.

We could heed the wise farmer who was not only successful in the planting and harvesting of his crops, but in cultivating his family ties. He believed his family as worthy of cultivation as the seeds he planted in the field. From his belief he reaped a rich harvest of love and respect. He was conscious that the required finesse was not a thing born within him, but that he must cultivate a love for the good, the true, and the beautiful.

Heads and hands can be purchased but hearts are cultivated. They are cultivated according to the nature of the individual. It is the natural desire of man to want someone with whom he can talk at length and depth on any subject without fear of being scorned and without having a snare set to prove past failures or present shortcomings.

He cherishes someone with whom he can be affectionate for the sake of expression and to see a little jealousy to boost his ego. He likes someone whose busy times will not keep him from leaving a task to share a walk and companionship.

He recognizes a great need for privacy and solitude. There is nothing wrong with closed doors as long as the mind is open. A person sometimes needs to be alone with his God to discover who he, himself, has grown to be.

And he knows the importance of his personal pride and personal behavior. They not only reflect on his own person, but upon his mate, for beautiful is often not beautiful but well groomed.

Gentleness and kindness are requisites of his rich harvest. There is mutual respect, observing all that is holy in one another, believing with all the heart that this mate is the most unique and excitingly worth-while person, whole in his own right, capable of seeing beyond petty things, never crying over spilled milk, cultivating all that is dignity, loyalty, peace-fulness, humility, and the right to love graciously.

There is a season of gathering for all who have planted richly in love.

✻

There is a lack of good judgment in planting a thought where we would not have it grow roots. Why should we suggest something to someone if we did not expect him to think it true? It seems to be the natural tendency of human beings to call attention to their shortcomings before the very people they would prefer not to notice them. Usually this is done in the hope that they will be contradicted. And though the listener may graciously say it isn't true, there has been a seed of thought planted that will grow with the slightest encouragement.

Jealousy is a bad gardener. It asks for constant proof of love's continued growth until the thought becomes a sugges-tion for love to pause along the way. Growth does not come through demand, but by cultivation. And too often jealousy awakens the naïveté until it asks, "why not?" and succumbs to the suggestion.

It is true that we reap what we sow, for once there was a man who had a beautiful garden. When he was small he played there. Later he worked there, finding enjoyment in

seeing it progress and grow. But he did not really know how beautiful it was until he walked there with someone he loved. He made no explanation about how it had become so beautiful, nor about the weeds that had popped up from time to time, but only assured her that it was just as beautiful as it seemed. And they lived happily ever after.

Such is the medley of life.

＊

Autumn, and it is lovely! Everything has that fresh clean scent of night rain and of the wood smoke spiraling through the treetops. It is a time for mediating between summer and fall, a time for bringing the two together in a long peaceful season of harvest. This is the season for gathering in the Indian corn and planning for winter wheat, for man was made to use his head and hands to keep his heart happy. It is not just a time for harvesting grains and vegetables, but also for man to see the fruits of his work.

Too many people are waiting until the sun shines or until it rains, or for their ship to come in or the tide to change, and suddenly time is gone and none of those marvelous things has taken effect—because nothing had happened except the waiting. Waiting must be coupled with faith, and faith with work, for man to have his season of fruitfulness. And then his work does not cease, for he makes it a season of beginning again, the preparation for the coming season. Every season is lovelier than the last and begs us not to wait but to prepare and to make every season a season to be happy.

It is said that life and death a
Because we live essentially in
rally interested in learning a
never accepted or believed th
We are guilty of using the pow
blacken, to destroy, to maim—
there is so much unhappiness a

There have been many insta
talked another back from self-
been many instances when too
of their words to kill.

It is foreign to most people to
physically. But it becomes a way
to harass someone beyond his en

Our words can be our servants
we send out comes home again.
casting and receiving stations with t
Even our most casual conversation
we idly discuss illnesses, hardships,

An athlete, a wonderful, bright
source of strength the Scripture, ".
the Lord shall renew their strength

...gs as eagles; they shall run, and not be weary; and...
...walk, and not faint" and won in track competition...
...ge margin. In his jubilance he unthinkingly poured...
...houghts to his coach only to have his faith sadly...
...by laughter and ridicule.
...an be destructive and kill, if we allow it; there is...
...or it, but never in God's kingdom.

*

...me if along the way somewhere . . . I have killed...
...pes and dreams . . . with my own disbelief in every...
...od.
...ve me if I could not see with your vision the beauty...
...world and the infinite possibilities for peace.
...ve me my restlessness . . . that I could not pause on...
...h . . . to allow wisdom to come forth.
...ve me that I have not treated each new day . . .
...e same ultimate joy that you know . . . for another...
...to be worthy.
...ive me for not listening . . . when the very atmosphere...
...harged . . . with universal music . . . and ideas too...
...to grasp.
...give me my foolishness . . . that I have believed . . .
...only existed those things . . . which I could see and...

...give me that I have not thought . . . deeply enough...
...tside the limits . . . of the ordinary mind . . . to believe...
...vercome.
...rgive me that I have not sensed . . . the intense value...
...e . . . the infinitesimal beauty everywhere . . . in the...
...est to the most majestic of God's creation.
...rgive me that I have not said thank you.

Chapter 3

"A time to kill, and a time to heal. . . ."

Sometimes when the moon wanes low . . . and the stars have all the sky . . . I cannot help but wonder some . . . and ask the reasons why. . . . With all this glory here below . . . and heaven there above . . . why must we quarrel about small things . . . when we were made to love. . . . The great and small, the young and old . . . the beauty of this land . . . from mountaintop to valley low . . . the beating surf and sand. . . . There is a Life within it all. . . . As dear as dear can be. . . . It is the beauty in your face. . . . It is the light in me!

*

How sad that so many believe in a time to kill but so few believe in a time to heal. How sad that we do not believe that good can equal bad when faith in good makes it all powerful just as faith in bad makes it the stronger.

While man works eagerly to explore outer space and the wonders of worlds believed to be in existence, the world of inner man has hardly been touched. Usually he has no idea in which direction to go in search of it.

If only he could believe it, man has within his power the ability to heal himself of illnesses, both mental and physical, through his spiritual faith. He cannot only heal the mind and body but situations and circumstances. Healing is not miraculous, but man's ability to have enough faith is the miracle.

Every time he speaks of his inability to help himself, another score is placed on the wrong side. Every time he says faith won't work, something in his life suffers. And every time he becomes discouraged, he aids his enemy.

Healing begins in the mind for every situation. It begins by faith and clings tenaciously if given even half a chance. Healing is every bit possible. And it is every bit probable if only man will have the faith required to give it life and action.

*

There is great consolation in knowing that with time all things will be made right. Time is a great healer, and must be paid for with patience.

With time forgiveness becomes more true, and mercifully time aids in forgetting. Time allows the mind to mature, helps it to grow in wisdom, and stabilizes it in difficulty.

Time is eternity returning every thing to its rightful place,

23

giving to those who need it comfort, strength, joy, and a sense of belonging and well-being.

Time is an educator, teaching those who would learn, and revealing more of life to the learned. To recognize its value is to be steadfast, knowing that with time all things work together for the good of those who wait.

*

It seems we can walk through hell and high water, live like the devil, find God in the most unlikely places, and come out with a strange kind of music in life.

Are not human spirits supposed to be superior to those things which are created to live by natural laws? And yet we beat up the earth and disfigure its kind old face in every possible way. Still, it seems to have the innate ability to fill in the scars, heave up its growing powers and burst into miraculous blooms that even the most destructive man-made weapons have been unable to stop.

What courage this earth possesses and what faith! If only we as spiritual beings would return so quickly to living after we have faced difficulty. Most of us have seen sorrow face to face and have not had the courage to turn away so quickly. We nurse scars and expect others to go on tip toes in respect to what we've been through. But disappointments, hurts, and painful memories are not holy. There is nothing sacred about them, for can we say that such things are divinely ordained? Like a gnarled tree on which nature has placed limitations, we are sometimes made different, either visibly or invisibly, but is it a vile trick played on us by our Creator? And is there any more reason for us to believe we must quit living than there is for the tree to refuse to burst into an extraordinary display of life? In its picturesque way, it is often more distinctive than one lost in the forest.

There is evidence of beauty in the most desolate garden. It may take several seasons to mellow the scars, to melt away the deep chasms, but to boldly begin will invite all the right forces to join in and help. It is then that life's music is not so strange, but strong and vigorous in faith and work and very sweet in beauty. After all, anyone can quit because of limitations, but it takes a hero to rev up his courage to find the rhythm and melody to life.

Chapter 4

"A time to break down, and a time to build up. . . ."

Forget, forget they all advise . . . no one should make you cry . . . forget there ever was a time . . . a memory to make you sigh . . . forget the stars and moon and sun . . . forget the time of day . . . forget the very thought of him . . . forget they always say . . . but I can still remember . . . such things are slow to fade . . . and I shall not forget this too . . . there are changes to be made . . . I cannot waste more time today . . . I cannot weep or sigh . . . whatever more is there to say . . . must surely be good-by!

Man fears change. He would wade through adversity, and strain under nearly impossible burdens rather than accept the idea of change. It is the general belief that if something has worked well in the past it will serve the same purpose in the future. But the wise man will recognize there is a time to break down and a time to build up. He has spent a lifetime collecting ideas, impressions, and false conceptions of himself and other people. If he is to go forward there comes a time when he must tear down those ivory towers he has built to this and that and begin all over again.

A survey of history will show the rise and fall of everything except God, the only unchangeable and dependable part of living. But to the person who has great pride in clinging to his ideas it seems absurd to even consider his way of doing things outmoded. He will cling to the old ways until they break him rather than accept a better way that would benefit him and all those who look to him for the values of life. Significant discoveries of lost civilizations prove that man alone will break first. Archaeological finds show centuries-old structures, pottery, cisterns, and even articles of clothing belonging to man whose way of life broke down too soon.

Man builds an idea within himself believing it to be what

others think of him. And though he knows it to be unstable, he will cling to it rather than brave a change. It matters immensely to him what others think, and he believes he knows what their ideas of him are. Laboring under this misapprehension he lives a lifetime in a house built on sand. The courage to break down and rebuild does not come easily. It takes great strength, great vision, and strong hearts.

It is the glory of a man to be able to examine within his own heart the person he really is. Here he dares to be painfully honest with himself. Here he can break down all the false fronts, all the vain images of himself, and bring out that inner person hidden under layers of pretension, fear, ignorance, and self-pity. Only by recognizing his own inner spirit can he rebuild.

Henry van Dyke had a saying, "Every house where love abides and friendship is a guest, is surely home." Man must feel love and friendship within the confines of his own being before he can show it outwardly. His home is his own making. Whether it is large or small makes no difference but the quality of the person within determines the kind of outward person. A serene household is a reflection of one who has loved, has good thoughts, and knows contentment. A chief cornerstone in his household is the ability to laugh and enjoy. A well-protected household is one that can close the door in the face of deceit, gossip, and indignity, for the decor cannot be one of elegance if the interior is crumbling. It was Seneca, speaking in the manner of the Stoics, who said, "It is true greatness to have in one the frailty of a man and the security of God." And the courage to break down so to build up.

*

In the summertime, the river is warm, still, and hardly wet. Huge trees hang over the water and drop dead branches and yellow leaves on the almost motionless surface. An occasional flip of a fish's tail sends out a ripple and a swarm of water bugs ski across the hazy overlay. The murky liquid moves even less where the banks recess and debris clogs drainage so that mosquitoes and other insects have a place to breed in their most prolific manner. Along these areas, navigation is impossible except by a small, flat-bottomed boat that can be moved with an oar. A larger boat with power to go the whole distance must keep to the center of the river where the flow is free and open.

There is a river of life that flows through the existence of every man and woman. The stream is wide and backs into every nook and cove, trapping itself in shallow pools and low, swampy places until it becomes stagnant. Here it forms a cover or a scum that attracts impurities and narrows down the actual flow of the river to a ribbonlike stream at the very center. This is the only fresh, uncontaminated water in the whole life. Here is the way, "the strait that is very narrow and few ever find." It is the ceaseless flow that washes away anything unlike itself. It is the only part that keeps free of the snags and blocks along the edges of the mind or of the life. Too many streams of life believe they are supposed to find quiet little coves and stagnate. This is the way it has always been done, all the formal training for life to be in a certain place at a certain time, searching out no new routes to allow a fresh rivulet the opportunity of becoming a fine clean flowing stream. Following along in the washes and gullies that have been cut before and before and before, it is pursuant to established form and is looked upon with disdain if it overflows its banks. There is little hope that all these little obstructions along the edges of the mind or life will break up on their own accord. They are trapped and stagnant before they have hardly become a part of the mainstream. Their only hope is that the over-all season will so change that the stream will rise above itself and break loose the outmoded tradition and give it new life.

Every young person in building his or her life should know how important it is to keep the center stream clear and free flowing. He should know that all along the way are nooks and coves that will beckon him to come in. If the lay of the land is lower than that which is required for him to flow out again, he is trapped. He is trapped until there is a breakup, and breakups can be very savage, tearing loose the set patterns and the tangled emotions. They can muddy the water and rile the grime, and only time will move the whirlpools and eddies out into the mainstream to be washed away.

All along the way are calm, peaceful-appearing pools that say, "Here is your nook, your cove, here is the fulfillment for which you have been searching and there is nothing better on down the way." There will even be times when it seems the mainstream is forcing parts of itself into the stagnant places, so there is required a constant awareness, a constant struggle to stay in the flow. But the struggle will be less if the mind is alert and can avoid the traps set for it. It takes a constant stimulation of the flow, which comes only from the inner mind and spirit, to look past the subtle invitations to linger a moment and to stay in the strait where the water flows cleanly and freely on its way to the great whole, the rolling, tumbling, lively freedom of the sea.

*

Emerson once said that the world exists for the education of each man.

One person, one creed, one group cannot have all the answers. What has been compiled into formulas and rules must be discovered over and over again by individuals searching for themselves. Everything that is, or will ever be, has always been. Man is merely discovering or rediscovering. But if he ever stops searching, all is lost.

The world is a thousand educations to a thousand searchers. We need them all to keep the balance. And in that balance there is unity, so many different, yet so alike. When we realize the importance of the other person to our own education we shall find something on which to begin building, instead of hunting ways to be destructive.

*

Some things can be mended and some we must tear down and begin again.

As a race of people who even now stands too close in memory to a time when there was little with which to accomplish even daily goals, there is a definite need to get rid of the old to make room for the new. To build a home, space must be made available by clearing away rubble and making way for the basic work to begin.

One suggestion toward solving the world's social problems has been to rebuild slums. The slums have already been built. There is a need for real homes. But before we see sunshine and geraniums in our most poverty-stricken areas, we will all have to change within ourselves. Poverty, like everything else, is partly a state of mind. A friend once expressed delight because someone about whom she felt deep concern had finally exchanged his old jalopy for a nice automobile. But she added quickly, "He won't be happy until it looks just like the old one."

Some of the world's most affluent people have poverty-stricken beliefs, whether it is money sewed in a mattress, or the feeling that it is wrong to have any money at all. We cannot say to be poor is a holy thing as long as it breeds ignorance and crime, or anything that keeps us all from being decent, well-adjusted human beings. It doesn't mean that everyone who is poor is poverty stricken. Many who are without sufficient funds live well and happily, while others with a constant inflow of resources live in absolute squalor. Poverty runs much deeper than material possessions. It involves the mentality, the spiritual life; and never let it be said that the spiritual life has nothing to do with finances. It has all to do with them. Educating a poverty-stricken person to accept something, keep it in good condition, make it increase in value, and gratefully share it, will take years—perhaps more years than the individual is willing to give. But help an individual to know himself as good, to know himself as a spiritual being, to give him a sense of security and worthiness, then his education can come quickly.

There is something about discovering we are more than just complex combinations of nerves, muscles, and appetites that makes us want to learn every good thing about ourselves and thus about all mankind. It makes us want the world to know it can be better than it ever dreamed it could be.

It is constructive to encourage man to help himself. He must feel the accomplishment of his own efforts to live fully and freely. There is a profound lesson in the simple act of feeding the birds when a heavy snow makes it impossible for them to find food. When the snow is gone, the birds still expect the food to be thrown to them, though they are able to find it for themselves.

There is truth in the fact that when financial troubles come in the door love flies out the window, unless we believe in something greater than a temporary pinch. A poor person with vision is not poverty stricken. A poor person who believes in himself, believes in God, and believes in God in others will not long remain poor.

We need to break down the slums in the hearts and minds and souls of people and build up beliefs in good, in worthiness, in pride as a sense of gratitude, in honest work, and

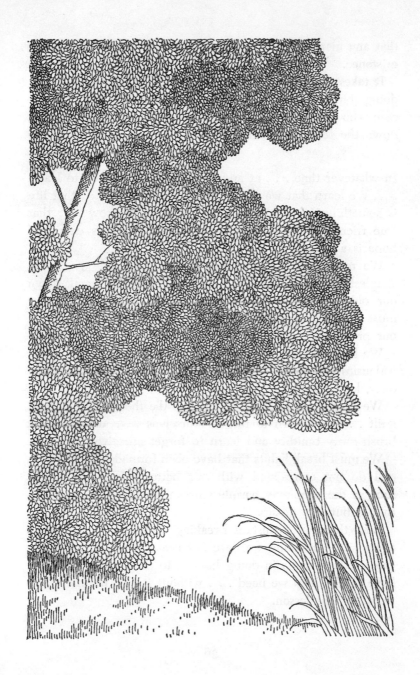

that any man can take one good idea and rebuild his entire existence.

It takes a person who believes, a person who believes in doing things for himself, and in doing so lifts others up—a man who knows how to make room for success by breaking down the fears and building up the faith.

＊

In whatever time . . . at any age we have so much to learn. . . . We learn that we can be lonely in a crowd . . . that life is something in which we must continue to grow . . . that true friends are very precious . . . that peace is dear and hope is a necessity.

We must learn to be temperate . . . to find joy in the simplest things . . . that sometimes we have to break down our old ways in order to build better ones . . . that we must stop crying with the world . . . and start laughing at our problems. . . .

We have to learn to rise above petty things . . . rise above jealousies and envies and greed . . . and build instead generosity, loving kindness, and gentleness. . . .

We must learn to break away from the thought of constant guilt . . . and learn to forgive ourselves . . . and we must brush away timidity and learn to forget ourselves.

We must break habits that have been formed gradually . . . and do not correspond with our better selves . . . habits such as the seemingly harmless exchange of information . . . that is but idle gossip.

Life, then, is a constant breaking down and building up again . . . something we dare not cease to do . . . and the greatest help to us in doing both is to pray . . . with it we have all the help we need . . . without it . . . no one wants to know that lesson.

Chapter 5

"A time to weep, and a time to laugh. . . ."

The best of life to you, my dear . . . may all your dreams come true. . . . And though you planet hop, my dear . . . your friends will not be few. . . . Your effervescent smile, my dear . . . is your pass to everywhere . . . no matter where you go, my dear . . . you'll never have a care. . . . So pack your bag with joys, my dear . . . and scatter them as you go. . . . There are riches there for you, my dear . . . at the end of the next rainbow. . . . Climb aboard the wings, my dear . . . survey your world and sigh . . . but never say good-by, my dear . . . or I am apt to cry!

Can I pray that my children will never have reason to cry? Is it wisdom to wish them that?

I remember some of my own tears. I have cried because someone loved me, because I loved someone, because I was not loved. I have cried in anguish, in fear, in illness, but most gloriously when I realize I am not alone in my private world. I have something that neutralizes bitterness and cleanses from my mind and heart the scars and smudges that have caused me to cry.

Tears are of the soul and if I had never cried I would not know the depths of my being or the purification of even the memory of times and circumstances that have ruled with unbending fury.

I have cried from relief just knowing a tremendous burden was being lifted, felt the tension and rigidity of something that was not faith being dissolved away.

· Joy and relief are sometimes too deep for laughter and cannot be quieted by adding more joy but only by weeping them back to livingness.

To cry for pain or illness or frustration is not an emotion that heals or that comes from any real depths. Only a calming peacefulness can give relief, a peace that comes from letting go to faith. It is necessary to rise above the emotions and not let them dominate until hysteria rules common sense.

Tears are a fulfilling emotion but they are not weapons to be used idly and for the purpose of making demands. They are God's own purifying force capable of greatness.

O that I should be so foolish to ask never to let my children cry, but only that it be more for love and joy than for sadness.

*

Have you never laughed to save face, to cover an embarrassing moment, to ease someone else's self-consciousness?

Someone very great once wrote that next to love a good sense of humor was our greatest gift. Our ability to laugh, to find subtle humor in the meanest things, can make them less ominous, less apt to grow into monsters. Oliver Wendell Holmes used to say that laughter and tears were meant to turn the same machinery of sensibility; one windpower and the other waterpower. And certainly there is power in both.

The most fretful mind can ease the pain by laughing in forgetfulness of self, allowing it to roll from the depths to stretch the tight little inner person. A hearty laugh not only aids digestion but makes a meal a feast. It breaks the gloom like sunlight and falls like glittering prisms of color across the heart.

To laugh is healthy. It never allows one to take life so seriously that it becomes a burden. God gave us wit and humor that we might be able to step aside from the serious self and poke a little fun in a delightful way to keep rhythm and spirit working together.

Life is a co-operative experience. It demands a great deal of us, but it also supplies the balancing factors to help us bear the demands. Frequently, these equalizers are called tears.

There seem to be special times for tears. Although we ordinarily think of them as results of unhappiness, this is not always true, for there are many good reasons for tears. Sorrow is easier to bear with tears, but tears are also for beauty. To some, the songs that remind them of other times that were meaningful can stir their hearts to deeper feeling. Tears can be for a love so beautiful that only God could have created it. Tears can also accompany laughter when your heart overflows with joy.

For whatever the reason, whether or not there is a sadness or a sweetness to tears, the deeper their meaning, the greater our capacity for living. And for all the reasons we may shed tears, probably the most frequent reason is from sheer frustration. It seems we condition ourselves for the major things, but frustration comes more often and in so many different ways it is difficult to pinpoint its beginning and control it. And so comes a flood of tears to relieve the tension and stress. They are not signs of weakness but have in themselves a cleansing that washes away hurt, humiliation, and yes, sometimes bits of old love that no longer hold a place in the heart.

There is great truth that weeping may endure for the night but joy comes in the morning. And so it is true that the darkness before the dawn tends more to tears and yet ushers in a more refreshed and more meaningful dawn when we can find humor in our most anxious thoughts. For in the light of day our difficulties are not so ominous and we are not so terribly and seriously involved with ourselves. We come to a place where we can see what humorous combinations of mixed emotions, beliefs, disbeliefs, thoughts, and behavior we can really be and we learn there is something about laughter that heals too. To include a good measure of laughter in one's daily routine is a must. It should be a part of each course at the dinner table, a sharing of the happenings of the day with the ability to laugh at oneself. Sharing laughter with others who enjoy exercising their God-given ability to enjoy their humor produces an exhilarating sense of joy.

Laughter is contagious. The solemn find themselves smiling and the cheerless cheerful. There is simply something about it that shakes the dark spots out of us, as Henry Ward Beecher has so thoughtfully written, "Mirthfulness is in the mind, and you cannot get it out. It is the blessed spirit that God has set in the mind to dust it, to enliven its dark places, and to drive asceticism, like a foul fiend out the back door." We who are so splendidly organized to feel unhappy sometimes find our sense of humor too frail. Spontaneous laughter can lift a sad heart and mend a broken one. The very sound of it carries a message to the world that there is still something about which to laugh. The greatest message of all is the sound of laughter to little children. To them it means security, that all is well. We need to share our laughter with them, to inspire them to see the humor in the most serious conditions and to help them know that happiness is a part of their legacy.

God gave us the ability to laugh as he gave us the ability to cry. We can no more spend all our time in tears than we can in laughter, but joy is often an instigator for tears just as laughter can wash away a painful memory—making always a time for weeping and a time for laughter—and all in God's good time.

Yes, there is a time to cry. We should cry when we are less than we could be. It isn't easy to be a whole person and there may well be tears of frustration, but to be a whole person, to have feelings deep enough for tears, is a giant step. It is when we become so blasé that tears seem ridiculous that we are in danger of breaking from sheer dryness.

Jesus wept, God forbid that I cannot.

*

There are extremes and opposites in every life. There are highs and lows, rights and wrongs, tears and laughter, and somewhere in between we try to find a happy medium. But try as we do, sometimes we go to the extremes and find the way back to normalcy no small job to accomplish. It is a difficult situation with which to live and nearly impossible to explain to those who try to understand but cannot for many reasons.

It was author Christian Nestell Bovee who thoughtfully stated, "Tranquil pleasures last the longest. We are not fitted to bear long the burden of great joys." Nor are we fitted to live in turmoil and disappointment without having them leave emotional scars that are difficult to remove. To strike a balance is a continuous job that requires wisdom and even kindness and understanding toward one's self and to others. It is not always accomplished alone and never without God.

*

What is a friend? Someone with whom we can share our problems? Our private disposal for worries, fears, and hurts?

The adage, "Laugh, and the world laughs with you; weep, and you weep alone" is sometimes painfully true. There is nothing more wonderful than friends when we need them, but to weight them down with our frustrations and then turn a sunny face to a mere acquaintance is a breach of friendship.

If there is anything our friends need it is a kind word, an understanding that they cannot always bear our burdens on top of their own. Everyone has obligations to meet, and it is wrong to believe that because someone is a good friend we should do nothing but unload our troubles on him. A friend is indeed a friend who has borne this weight without going out to find a more cheerful person with whom to spend a happy hour.

It is unnatural to never find a chuckle to share, to be forever long-faced and without a sense of humor. A wise person knows the joy of a good laugh and the spirit of fun. If man had everything, but did not have the sense to enjoy it, there would be little use of having anything. Life without a smile is a mere existence.

Hawthorne declared, "A stale article, if you put it in a good, warm, sunny smile, will go off better than a fresh one that you've scowled upon."

We need often to dip our sense of humor in a few refreshing thoughts to insulate ourselves against life's stale ideas.

We need to learn how to laugh, if only at ourselves.

Chapter 6

"A time to mourn, and a time to dance. . . ."

Though April may bring you a shower or a flower . . . a rainbow of every hue . . . though the sun may touch your nose or your toes . . . happiness depends on you. . . . Love may come with a flair or with care . . . or whistle a tune for your ear. . . . And whether the sound be a joy or annoy . . . depends upon how you hear. . . . Life waits for no one, nor hurries away. . . . It's there for the choosing, you see. . . . Whether April or May . . . or whatever the day . . . it's that which you make it to be!

Life is sometimes interrupted in the way that a room is when wind thrusts open the shutters and fills it with fresh air and a bit of new living. Some outside force must push its way into our lives or we might go on forever living in musty attics and dark undeveloped minds.

We should always look on seemingly adverse situations as those which have come to awaken us and to bring into our lives a more meaningful and fuller living. It isn't easy to give up those things that have become a part of us. We love the familiar touch, the familiar scents, the familiar sounds but these sometimes demand their freedom and though it leaves us bewildered it also leaves a message. That message is that here is a new life, a new challenge, and if we are made of the right stuff, if we can find the grit and determination to follow a way that has been given to us and make it count for something, we have taken the handles to plow a new furrow.

We are never alone, for those whom we have loved are with us, urging us on to new and better things. Those whom we shall know and love are waiting along the way to give direction and to stretch forth a hand to help us over the places that are unfamiliar.

Life demands that we step past self-pity and pick up the

loose ends of our lives and begin the weaving process that will eventually, as quickly or as slowly as we choose to work, make a stronger fabric of life. A constant questioning, regret, and remorse over thought of failure are not a part of the God of life. If we were to lay life aside because of our losses we would be a disappointment to our Creator. We would be made of inferior material with areas of weaknesses that could not be depended upon. The silver flagon of life that is full to overflowing goes to the person who has the ability to see God in every situation.

＊

I grieve so for little things. I wonder sometimes why I allow the small things to become so important that I am hurt when they are destroyed or damaged. Especially when there are so many truly important things such as life and limb and soundness of mind. Yet, I find myself having a personal acquaintance with the dearness of a book, a vase, a figurine, all so unimportant to those who need bread and joy and comfort. But to give the necessities of life one must be capable of loving the great and the little, to be capable of understanding, to have a desire to comfort, a need to share the small things, and to have a sense of oneness with the beauty in a thing or a person. Small things inspired the English novelist Bulwer to comment, "There is so little to redeem the dry mass of follies and errors that make up so much of life, that anything to love or reverence becomes, as it were, a sabbath to the soul."

Perhaps when we grieve we know we are capable of loving, and that indeed is a sabbath to the soul.

＊

No man can truthfully say that at some time in his life he has not made a foolish decision. But man cannot quit living

because of a false move or even many false moves. He gets up, dusts himself off, and goes right on—ever in search of the right way, but never allowing the present and future to be prisoners of the past.

Frequently it is the thought that when there has been a sad mistake there should also be a mourning period. Though regret seems inevitable, it is not to live with, nor should we even briefly park by it. There can be mountains of thought and worry and if-onlys, but there are also new and more excellent heights to which a man can rise to overcome them. All of us can do it if we can grow big enough to lay aside regrets, lay aside distrust, hard feelings, and self-pity and get to work on the answer and allow the problem to dissolve.

Chapter 7

"A time to cast away stones, and to gather stones together. . . .

*I stood out under the stars last night . . . and wondered
each small light . . . could shine upon this earth so dark
could swell and blaze, glitter and spark . . . just show
man the way to go. . . . They pattern the sky that he mig
know . . . the order and rhythm of nature's way . . . tha
man might join with man someday . . . and make a light
within his mind . . . a tenderness for all mankind . . . an
inner joy that shall cast out . . . the meanest things that make
men doubt!*

It is said that during the peaceful times in ancient years the vineyard keepers gathered together stones from among the grapevines and piled them in fence rows. Their time was free to do an orderly work and the vineyards were clean and highly productive. But during the years when they were ininvolved in wars, the stones were cast about, symbolic of the disorder that comes with conflict, unrest, and lack of discipline.

Man is still making a time for gathering stones together and he is still casting them away. When he is quiet and at peace with himself, his affairs are orderly and easily made productive and valuable. But when he has inner conflict and a lack of self-discipline, he carries with him burdens of hopelessness and self-condemnation and there is no constructive work. The very thing within him serving as his livelihood is so mistreated and so neglected that it wilts and slowly dies.

A beautiful garden is a rewarding sight. It shows the touch of loving hands. And it is marvelous to see another person with the inner glow of an excellent nature from careful cultivation of his deeper self. This person has taken the time to gather together all the symbols of hard feelings, all resentment, and hardships and has unloaded them from his back.

He is no longer reminded of whom he found unjust, or un-friendly or unco-operative. These thoughts no longer do him injury by hanging like millstones about his neck to remind him that there ever was a time for gathering stones together or a need for casting them away.

*

He's just a little man. His hat is a bit askew as he walks slowly and thoughtfully. He pays little attention to the world about him, and sometimes in general conversation his language lacks something to be desired. Frequently, he is smiled upon because of his eccentricities, but that does not bother him a bit. He knows where he has been and he knows where he is going—which is decidedly an improvement over most of us.

You see, unless you take time to know him, you would never guess that a giant of a man walks within him. His kindness, his financial aid, whatever he has is there to help when someone truly needs it. Many persons have been in his debt. He has never once asked for repayment.

The park bench is a favorite retreat and the squirrels are his friends. He has a deep and abiding love for nature, and he has as deep a desire for kindness and attention as any man. Let us not pass him by without seeing him twinkle with genuine good humor, even though he must wonder at human nature.

He is just a little man. He is a stone we dare not cast away for he is a diamond in the rough, a jewel in the rarest sense.

*

Unless you are a rock collector you probably would never notice the shape or size of a stone except for something obviously eye-catching. To most, rocks in general appear pretty much the same. But when a special stone has been tossed and thrown against other rocks we see they have an inner glow or beauty and are capable of being polished. These are the rocks that stand out from the others and are recognized for their value.

Are we so different from the stones? We offer little of life worthwhile to anyone until we have had a bump or two. Until we have been tossed and rained upon a few times, we have little incentive to prove life to ourselves or even to thank God for the opportunity.

Even the most precious and cherished stones must be polished and faceted to be gems. Often it requires the artistry of an experienced gemologist to bring out the true beauty and crystal clarity in a beautiful stone. But when that stone has passed through the period of cutting away and polishing with order and precision, then it can be placed in a setting worthy of all its beauty. From there it has the right to ride the crest of happiness as the symbol of love and devotion because it has lent itself well to the hands of the Master Artist.

*

My heart is the heart of a beachcomber, a lover of all the beautiful treasure that abounds along these shores. There is hidden treasure everywhere, rich treasure enough for everyone. To gather these precious stones requires a trained eye, a loving heart, and an alert and childlike spirit.

> Sun and sand and misty sea,
> Your sights and sounds are part of me;
> I am rich and loved and made anew
> Because I am a part of you!

With so many jewels to gather, my search begins at the first sign of the pink-tinted dawn. The tide has washed in and washed out again leaving behind its treasures from the deep. I love to sit on the sugar-white sand and examine the shells, each unique in its own exquisite way. The one I cradle in my hand is lined with mother of pearl. My heart goes out to the oyster for the lesson of life it relates to me by turning its hurt into a thing of beauty, a priceless pearl. the morning light catches in the iridescent hollow of the shell, changing the colors to the depth and beauty of the richest opals. It is here that I gather my first gems.

As the sun climbs higher, I walk on so not to miss the blue sapphires and aquamarines as they glitter and dance on the crest of the waves and fall in a shower to caress my face. In the dazzling white light of sun and sand, the sea tosses mist high and drops diamonds to adorn my sun-kissed fingers and toes. And by high noon the sun is nudged away by one small angry cloud with the tropical temperament to throw torrents of rain to soak the hot sand. Everything but the pelicans runs for cover. But they, like great, gray, floppy umbrellas, fly lazily along spotting fish and diving madly into the foaming surf.

Sandpipers pitter-patter up and down the water's edge catching the golden glow like topaz after the storm. Evening falls as the sand crabs in their fierce attire come out to tumble and play like children in the sand. Along the horizon there are rubies glowing like live coals and turning the sunset to rich tints of amethyst and many shades of violet.

It is suppertime and my day has been a mental and spiritual experience of great wealth. In the quiet moments of this day I have watched the sand drift like time to cover the broken shells of broken dreams. And in its drifting it has also uncovered driftwood and memories that should have remained buried.

Retracing my steps along the shore I feel the tide again washing in, washing the sand from beneath my feet, reaching

higher and higher on the shore to bring in a new treasure for tomorrow.

Away from the sea, evening settles on the hills and rolling meadows with all hues of precious emeralds that whisper of still waters and green pastures. The night, like onyx solitude, falls in sweet rest and is softened by silver moonlight. It is now that all creation, land and sea and precious stones, are gathered together in infinite peace.

*

Too many times we punish ourselves for our yesterdays. We consider a long time what today might have been had we chosen a different route. All the days past are determining for us what today will be as it passes moment by moment.

Our lives are lived in many stages, but it is up to us to make each moment count since it does serve as tomorrow's foundation. Our pasts may not have been faith and good works, but we can wipe out those mistakes the moment we forgive ourselves and others and begin to live in the present. Neither can we rest on our laurels, for as long as there is life there is work to be done. We do not eat one time and sleep one night and make it last for a lifetime.

So many people give thought, strength, and belief to bad as being equally as powerful as good. In doing so they create unbelievable barriers they cannot cross. Their very lives then become absorbed in ritualistic effort to escape those things that return again and again to torment and twist meanings and definitions of life's simplest problems. They are surrounded and plagued with infinite uncertainty and therefore are prey to continual fears and anxieties from which it seems impossible to escape. It drains them of normal thought and action and soon they can practice nothing but mental pictures of wrong and dire consequences, and thus the ritualistic effort to flee from it.

When man can see his God as love and all good, and all good only, and give his complete thought to the knowledge and affirmation of this, his mental attitude will release those things that once held him spellbound, and the thing that plagued him will melt into the nothingness from which it came. It requires patience and intestinal fortitude to dispose of the past. Our worries and fears do not all go at once, sometimes they have to have the second and third match.

Chapter 8

"A time to embrace, and a time to refrain from embracing. . . ."

*How often in the early morn . . . when all the world is new
. . . I stand and gaze at the rising sun . . . and my thoughts
will turn to you. . . . Are you happy? Is life worthwhile?
. . . Are your hours too few? . . . Do you mind when the day
is done . . . that your dreams have not come true? . . . Do
you weary of all the things . . . that life demands each day?
. . . Can you find a quiet place . . . apart in which to pray?
. . . And do you leave time . . . between morn and night . . .
some time just to be free? . . . But more than that I want
to ask. . . . Do you ever think of me?*

Timing is of essence in any venture, but never more so than in choosing the persons and possessions that make up our everyday lives. We are eager to embrace that which touches our emotional nature, eager to possess that which seems to be ours, because we have already claimed it in our minds and hearts. But claiming is not enough without wisdom.

Early-day clergyman Charles Simmons once wrote that many things lawful are not expedient. Effectual and compatible living is merely common sense, moving when it is expedient and not just when lawful.

We have been reminded time after time that "fools rush in where angels fear to tread," and man is foolish when he tries to avail himself of all that the eye and mind accepts before the appropriate time. It may be entirely within the boundaries of his "rights," of which man is so overly conscious, but insisting on the right of way before the way is clear is dangerous business. The freedom or rights of one must cease where he begins to abuse the freedom or rights of another.

Man would have perfection where he invests less than his best. He would claim skill and experience and yet conceal his lack of fulfillment, for the race goes not to the swift, nor the battle to the strong, or the favor to men of skill, but to the wise in timing.

Timing in all phases of human behavior is of such import that the writer of Ecclesiastes asks why man strives so after the wind. Certainly there has been much striving after wind in the personal lives of man, but nowhere is it more evident then in the affairs of the male and female.

The most ridiculous mistake a man can make is to believe woman thinks as he does. And woman in all her ethereal theories of love must know, if she is wise, that the romantic and mysterious atmosphere surrounding her is for the most part created by the fluttering of her own wings. For her love is largely psychological and minutely physical. She is more fully tuned to the smallest incident, fragrance, melody, and gentle glance than her male counterpart. Indeed, a compatible relationship may depend on one word, one passing thought or emotion. Though there are exceptions to every rule, the words of the poet Lord Byron still remain largely true, "Man's love is of man's life a thing a part, 'tis woman's whole existence." Therefore, every single act of the day, every thought and consideration, every joy and tear and action becomes a part of her love. They may work together or disrupt, for one small thing is relative to another, dictating to her emotions and actions, soothed, healed, and delighted only with greater and more constant love.

Man likes to feel he is loved and woman wants to be told. Woman must feel her part in the relationship as important. She doesn't enjoy what she considers a duty any more than a man wants to be chained to a responsibility. Even a dog that must be chained is not an ideal pet.

Adversity is not so much the foe of man and woman, but more frequently the lack of ability to love and understand and to have the good sense to know there is a time to embrace, and there is a definite time to refrain from embracing.

66

＊

Everyone wants to be wanted. It is frightening to lose contact with other people even in our thoughts. It makes us lonely, and loneliness is something we would just as soon not know about or care to investigate. It preys on the busiest while he stands alone in a swishing, moving throng of humanity. We long to be near those with whom we can be quiet, laugh, talk, and not worry about being an outsider.

Loneliness would have us think we are on the outside of the land of the living. It would have us think no one cares, that life, the happy, pulsing, living kind, does not exist and even if it did it would not include us.

Loneliness is an alarm to warn us that we have cut ourselves off from other people. There are hundreds of lonely people every place waiting for a smile and a friendly voice. If there be a time to lose, let it not be here where so many need so many. We need to break out of our shells, to reach out a hand, to involve ourselves in seeing that someone else is not lonely and our loneliness will disappear!

Everyone wants to be wanted! And there is no better way to seek than by attracting, attracting a friend by being one!

＊

Can any other person take what belongs to me? Not if it is really mine.

We are professionals when it comes to complaining about what others have taken from us. It is unfortunate that we do not realize the impossibility of taking what belongs to someone else. To lose someone's affection is possible, but to have it taken is impossible. We must have first lost it by our indifference or complacency, or even by our dominating influences.

Ignorance has caused great unhappiness and has closed the doors of communication that make understanding possible, thus forfeiting many times the very things we do not believe it is possible to lose. (There is nothing material that gives us assurance that anything of life is totally our own.) Only that which is in the heart and soul, only that invisible something that says my own belongs to me.

*

If there is ever anything or any time in your life to make you think "there must be a better way," it is when you first begin learning about human nature. Competition runs high among the young and increases in tempo as time goes by. The first defeat is a disillusioning experience, but one you never forget if you are very wise.

It is possible to spend one whole afternoon building a clubhouse out of hard native lumber and be called home to supper just before the dedication ceremonies. Following the beaten path through the orchard, you suddenly hear the voices of your friends calling you and in the true sense of comradeship you take a chance on being late and feeling the switch to answer that call, only to hear, "Yoouu don't b'lonnng to our club any more!" It isn't so much the work you put in, nor the exclusion from such an active society, but it is just the principle of the thing. Was it a social blunder to leave before the president made his speech, or is there just a sneaky little suspicion that this is a part of human nature, this power to put someone on the outside for the sheer fun of exercising that power?

Is it human nature, the mark of the race, to receive eagerly those who can benefit us and exclude them when they have served a purpose; only to embrace them again when a new game starts or the old members of the club fall out and there is a need for new blood to take sides?

Maybe we should not stop to answer when we are skipping through the orchard of life for fear our membership in the

human race has been canceled. But no, we have to take the small disappointments in our stride and hurry on to the feast of real living. We can't lose time or worry about who the instigator of such a plot might be, for he has only set in motion his own disinheritance by wishing it on another.

It takes only a few years in the beginning of life to know there are times you embrace your friends and times when you refrain from embracing them—or even from helping them build a clubhouse.

Chapter 9

"A time to seek, and a time to lose. . . ."

You have not dreamed until you've dreamed . . . a childhood dream, you see. . . . You haven't thought a happy thought . . . or know just how to be . . . a king or queen or circus clown . . . or a forest ranger brave. . . . You haven't lived a real life . . . until you've dug a cave . . . and you have to climb the old ash tree . . . and spin a cowboy rope . . . but more than that and all these things . . . you must know how to hope . . . and believe with all your childhood heart . . . and never once confuse . . . a grown-up fear with a childhood dream . . . for childhood dreams can't lose!

Drama in real life has often put to shame the creative abilities of the most gifted playwright. The unique and sometimes wholly unusual turns that real life takes in its daily revolution would be hard to swallow if we saw them on the stage. And this may well be the reason there is a frequent dipping into the bag of suggestive and provocative scenes that seem more believable on the stage than strange and thought-provoking truths. With this knowledge then, we should not be too astounded when the dramatic essence of getting and losing, or winning and defeat, suddenly exchange places but not titles. It doesn't matter what we call the results, for the getting or the losing is all in the feeling—our conscious awareness of whether we have won or lost.

We cannot lose what is truly ours and we cannot lose that which does not belong to us in the first place, so where is the loss? It is in the mind and thought and attitude, in the belief that because one door closes there are no others to open. Some of the greatest losers of all time are those who supposedly won. And some of the most gracious losers have turned defeat into such significant gains as to surpass even the original trophy.

Since life is truth and truth is foursquare, we must know that everything is balanced out with something. It is difficult to detect at times, but as Emerson wrote in his essay on compensation, "We cannot part with our friends. We cannot let our angels go. We do not see that they only go out that archangels may come in."

To lose any time always seems privation, but with time and with faith that all things do work together for good, we see that something was closed to us only that we could grow enough to accept something even greater. How often we do not realize that it is at this very point that we come to know who really is the true winner or loser.

*

There is always a time to seek those small instances in every life that makes it grow. Anyone can pinpoint a certain time or place that has served as the turning point to stretch the mind and thinking past that small beginning.

The ways to grow are without number if the person is alert and tuned to them. There are rich ideas in the simplest of conversations, beauty in a sunrise and a sunset, and understanding in a handclasp if only we can tap that great potential and move out of the vacuum that seems to hold us.

We must be watchful for opportunities. We must seek beyond our small personal desires to find anything of lasting value. When we seek only to satisfy ourselves, we become stagnant and sooner or later fall into a pattern of existing without a purpose.

The silent moments of meditation, the seeking of reason and purpose, are great sources of growth and will ever be valuable in the progressive person's life. The right to seek is one of the greatest of opportunities.

＊

An artist friend, falling into dialect, once said, "If I was the head of the world I'd say, 'where's the remotest place on earth? Take me there!'"

And if he were the head of the world perhaps he would be taken to a South Sea island where life is one long time of tranquillity seasoned well with trade winds, tropical fruit, soft music, and beachcombing. Or to the other extreme, it could well be miles and miles of rolling prairie where the only sounds are the wind singing in the grass, the soft lowing of a cow late in the evening while she picks her offspring out of the herd, which all look to human beings exactly alike, the soft swishing of the pony's hoofs on the deep meadow grass, or even his frightened "ha—rum—ph!" as he shies away from a white limestone shining in the moonlight. Occasionally he could hear a coyote or two as they make sounds like a dozen yipping in unison.

If he is to choose among the remotest places on earth, he may select a retreat where a cabin is nestled in a small clearing or in a cozy recess somewhere along the mountainside. He could listen to the wind in the pines and the cardinal's whistle, and he could fish in a lake so still it minimizes the mountain's reflection.

If he were a child, the remotest place in the world could be found by climbing a favorite tree, lying on his back in the tall grass on the point of the highest hill, sitting in a secluded spot behind a hedge, though it is only ten feet from the house, or fishing in a pond where there is nothing but sky to reflect.

Where is the most secluded place on earth? Man does not really know where to look, though he combs the earth for peace and quiet, he will not find it for it is within himself where God lives. This is the place of complete stillness, com-

plete and utter serenity. Only here is the warmth and glow
of a sunset or the fresh first things of morning and the love
of a lifetime. Here is the remotest place in the world, whether
you are head of the world, or a ten-year-old dreamer.

*

A person has almost to be grown before he realizes that not
getting what he wants does not mean he has lost something.
Frequently, it is just the opposite, for as children or grown-
ups we never quite get as much good out of something when
it is handed to us as we do when we have to create it ourselves. Most every child prefers jar lids and pots and pans
to fancier toys.

In the days when such unusual and colorful toys were nonexistent, it took an ingenious young man to make his own
toys. His racer car might not have been too streamlined and
the wheels may have been of various sizes so that in going
downhill the left rear wheel humped up a little every time
it turned, but the finished product was a source of pride and
certainly gave a feeling of great satisfaction.

After having known the swift action of a racer with four
different size wheels it was natural that such inspiration would
excite the creativity in the same young man to fly—if only a
kite. By using the method of trial and error and a little en-
gineering ability born within him, he set out to put together
a kite using his own pattern and dredging up the materials
from an apple box, a piece of belting, and some heavy news-
paper. Inside the belting, he found long pieces of heavy cord
that he knotted together and rolled into a ball the size of
his double fists. Then, splitting strips of white pine from the
apple box, he curved and fitted the pieces until it was a piece
of utter skill and craftsmanship—for a ten-year-old. The news-
paper was fitted to the frame and the tail was attached,
according to the speed of the wind and how high the flight

76

was to be. A message was attached just in case the twine didn't hold, and out she sailed, swaying and swinging back and forth with the lift and grace of one of Orville Wright's first creations.

Who is to say we lose when we do not get the thing we seek? Perhaps it is the greatest opportunity of a lifetime, the opportunity to create, to seek out the things at hand and to put them to use, to prove that we can do most anything we set our minds to? What more important lesson can we learn to serve us in later life when our very livelihood depends upon it? Indeed, sometimes to lose is to get the greatest gift, the chance to prove our genius!

Chapter 10

"A time to keep, and a time to cast away. . . ."

Hesper, Hesperus, Venus, Vesper . . . you're only an evening star. . . . For ages past, the old and young . . . have wondered what you are. . . . Faithfully there in the evening sky . . . never out of His view . . . twinkle and glow, mapping the sky . . . the way He created you. . . . I try to be a star on my own . . . to glow when the clouds are there . . . to continue to work when it isn't seen . . . to do my job and never care. . . . Though the world may not know . . . or seem to hear Job's stars as they sang at dawn. . . . I have my place, my job to do. . . . And for God we carry on.

What have you of life's beautiful things? A rainbow's shimmering hues when the shower has ended? A warm brown puppy in the sunlight? A mockingbird singing while a thin veil of clouds is drawn like misty curtains across the full moon; a playhouse where string stretched from tree to tree shuts out all invaders; children's laughter and the fluttering of wings in the birdbath? A breath of cool air; a drink of water; velvet sleep; an evening walk; a good book; and a feeling of well-being?

The best of life's beautiful things are still free. They are bits and pieces of the joyful things that become part of us, that stay in our memories like a child in a field of daisies, a friendly hand, a smile, a whisper, a prayer of thanksgiving. What are we that is not a fragment from a past happiness? What are we worth but what we collect of life's beautiful things?

There are mountains of memories stored away in our subconscious minds—memories of every conceivable kind on every conceivable subject that has ever been closely related to our lives since the beginning of our existence.

As normal and happy individuals we can recall many happy memories—memories that are so dear and delightful that we live them again and again to savor every drop of happiness because they can return in all their fullness and produce the same warm and delightful feeling they gave originally. We cherish these memories and keep them in our conscious thought as much as possible. But there are many, many memories we have long since buried with absolutely no desire to ever recall them under any circumstances.

If we can allow our unhappy memories to be peacefully forgotten they will never create a problem, but when we forcibly throw a heavy cover over those things we prefer not to remember because of their painful effect, we can expect them to do damage to us—usually without our knowing, such memories are the true culprits threatening our well-being. It does no good to simply dwell on the morbid memories since they are really not worthy of such cognizance. And too often they are kept and carried about as if they were something sacred to remind us that we once made a mistake. Such burdens are crosses of our own choosing for no one, least of all a kind and loving Father-Creator, would expect a life-long punishment—only the very narrow mind of a loveless human being could expect that. There are no great spiritual rewards for anyone who wastes his whole life being sorry. The rewards are for those who can forgive and overcome what may have gone wrong, and make life a full, beautiful, and well-rounded testimony of what it is to believe in good. All such unhappy memories and the equally unhappy pictures they have etched on our minds can be laid to their blessed rest to allow that which is good and reasonable and productive to come forth and do something worthwhile for a change.

When the past has been touched with things best forgotten and the victim carries the fears deep within his consciousness, that past with all its skeletons can resurge and recall every painful memory. The future seems tinged with the redness of

the past and any chance of happiness seems to fade away in the distance. It is a wonderful thing to know that we can leave behind the person that was not a child of God, but the shell of an old self that was never really us at all.

Each unhappy memory can be taken out, dusted, fumigated, and laid none too gently in the disposal for complete and utter dissolving. Then there is no longer any chance of it coming back to haunt and hurt us. Those things are gone forever and in their place is the very glorious presence of something much finer and much greater. No matter how hard skeletons of the past may try, they cannot matter because they are cast out and fade into the nothingness from which they came.

So come on into my house, dear spring, you are welcome. Come gently to us with warm rains and abundant sunshine. Come wearing your gayest colors and enter through the windows and doors and penetrate our very thoughts that we too may know a rebirth and a newness of life.

We hope you will find us ready to receive you for there is much to do in preparation. We must polish the windows to let in the true light of understanding, we must sweep out the old dust and cobwebs from our thinking, and make room for exuberant, active ideas and happier times. We must air the rooms of our minds for there is a time to keep and a time to cast away.

Whatever doubts we may have, those doubts cannot overshadow that instantaneous feeling that though there may be some anxious moments, all is well.

It is very difficult when those we love are not by our side so that we can see they are in good health, well, and protected at all times. We tend to be more capable of thinking fearful thoughts about them than we are the stronger and better thoughts of protection and love. We are so prone to think negatively, as if our presence with them could possibly make a difference.

If we are ever to have faith and to utilize it to the fullest degree, it is at the times when unthinking persons suggest dire pictures to our minds. We have to know what to listen to and what to throw out as mere prattle. There are simply those persons who do not have the capacity to know that God's love transcends time and space and war and sets up a profound and loving protection and peace that we could not provide were we by their side.

In the face of every worrisome talker let us know that his thoughtless comments and disillusioned thinking is not a reality but only the result of his not yet having learned how to cast out of his mind every single negative thought that comes to it.

Chapter 11

"A time to rend, and a time to sew. . . ."

Away in the deep of the silver night . . . I heard a nightbird sing. . . . I knelt by the window in soft moonlight . . . and listened to him fling . . . his joyous notes of all his friends . . . the ones he learned by day. . . . And while they slept in feathered nests . . . he sang the night away.

He told of the joys of those who care . . . he said they would always know . . . no matter what the circumstance . . . that special place to go . . . to view the sunrise, to feel its rays . . . pierce the darkest night or day. . . . He sang, "Have faith, have faith, my friends . . . and your fears will melt away!"

Creativity is more often born of necessity than it is of genius. Making use of the simplest things at hand has more often provided a better life for those who chose to use their ingenuity instead of worrying about what they did not have. An inventive talent could lie dormant for a whole lifetime if it were not for the need of a person to satisfy his longing for food, for love, for beauty, and for a dozen other needs that make him seek answers.

A genius is not required in these lessons for living. But a natural flair is handy and an even larger amount of common sense and a simple determination can provide needed things the genius could not see. It takes a need and then the desire to satisfy that need.

There was a time when a lady sewed a fine seam without the aid of today's sophisticated machines. There simply came a time to sew and yes, a time to take out the stitches she so painstakingly stitched by hand. The materials were not always the silks and satins we read about, but rough fabrics, some bleached cottons and some unbleached. But they were serviceable and that was clearly important. Grandmother was such a woman. She was not one to mince words or waste her time. When curtain-making time came she set about stitching the ruffles along the edge until she came to the point of completion—the ruffles ran short and the curtain ran long. Her next move was to quietly but firmly gather the curtain on the edge of the ruffle. Her philosophy may well have been that when you ran out of the fancy stuff you use common sense—you use what you have, and she had curtain.

A perfectionist might well have said, "Oh, I couldn't live with that!" But we can never tell what we can really do until it comes our turn to be a perfectionist or use common sense.

To worry and fuss over what we do not have only holds it further in abeyance. But to make use of what we have at hand is to open the way to that for which we have a real need.

Reach out and make the stitches in the fabric of life. Ruffle it, if possible, but if the ruffles run short, waste no time in worrying about it, just rend it back a little and gather life up right there and stitch it down well—it will hold just fine until something better comes along.

*

There was a time when the art of homemaking was thought to be an absolute necessity to every young girl regardless of whether or not she aspired to the domestic life in her adult years. Through watching and doing she learned the culinary arts and the proper way to keep house, but more than anything else she learned to sew. The household linens, clothing, curtains, and mending depended upon her skill with the needle. As her formal education increased a new class in home economics was added to literature, grammar, and other subjects to develop her mind and ability.

The sweetest bouquet of posies should go to the young ladies who voluntarily undertake sewing projects for the sake of their Heads, Hearts, Hands, and Health. When one such

young lady was twelve she was the winner of a red ribbon for having put together the second-best dress at the county fair. It might well have been a blue ribbon except that she had to put this one together so many times.

Another bouquet should be presented to her mother for insisting the sewing be done right. Perhaps she did not insist once, but many times, the rending and sewing continuing until the dress at least reached the red-ribbon stage.

It makes little difference in which stage we are in life, whether we are sewing a seam or removing the mistakes, it is the doing and redoing that teaches us a rare lesson in excellence. If maturity teaches nothing else so plainly, it teaches us that we may as well do the job right in the first place. If we do not, it will return again and again for our correction and clarification until we learn that life is not pasted together with flour and water.

Try as we will to escape facing up to our responsibilities, we cannot avoid them. And it is a wise parent who does encourage a child to give his best at every turn so that he will never have to be satisfied with second prizes. Only then can he tie off all the loose threads and never have to look back in regret and wish he had tried harder. Rending will always be a part of life until the stitching is as near perfect as possible.

Chapter 12

"A time to keep silence, and a time to speak. . . ."

*Don't tell a soul I told you this . . . a secret must be kept
. . . and I wouldn't tell you not to tell . . . of what I said
except . . . that someone might tell someone else . . . and
what would I do then . . . but say that I don't know how
. . . or where, or who, or when. . . . For secrets are not meant
to say . . . who told them, don't you see . . . for if you said
a certain thing . . . it might get back to me!*

We learn so many good things from great souls, not always by what they talk about, but by their silence. There is often a more meaningful communication of understanding and trustworthiness in silence than in conversation.

There would be much less clamor if we could just stop talking soon enough. The plight of the human being is that he creates a mountain of disturbances and then tries to climb over it.

We seem to think nothing is working well for us unless we can see it, and to make up for what we cannot see, we talk about it until we create problems where none existed. When time is all spent talking there is no time for listening, and without new ideas talk is very cheap.

Robert Louis Stevenson said, "You start a question and it's like starting a stone from on top of a hill; away the stone goes, starting others." And so it is with talking, the first idle remark may foster others until the words all run downhill and cease to have meaning. Getting back to the silence that is golden is to start back up the hill.

❊

As all things tend to cease when we complain about them, relentlessly the spring rains stopped as if they were coming from the shower faucet and someone had flipped the handle. Perhaps they really stopped because it was no longer spring. But for whatever the reason, the lush green of the forest was suffering, first from too rapid growth that depended on a great amount of moisture and then from a complete and sudden lack of rainfall.

When I entered the woods the atmosphere was limp and wilted. Even the blue jay failed to stir up much excitement with his shrill warning cries. There was no breeze to ruffle the lacy fern fronds, and the red squirrel was stretched out on the limb of the elm tree panting from the close heat. Bird wings fluttered only fast enough to get them short distances from limb to limb or tree to tree.

I hoped that soon these creatures and these beautiful woods would be relieved from the heat, but how soon it was to happen seemed impossible to believe. A sudden gust of air swept through the underbrush stirring the leaves in all directions. For a brief moment there was complete silence but the wood-folk immediately sensed the change in the air pressure. They were alert and scurrying around chirping and chattering, in search of shelter or in the spirit of expectancy.

Following the path that only a frequent visitor would know existed, I walked deeper into the woods. A sharper wind touched the treetops tossing them violently, this time accompanied by a low rumble of thunder. Grapevines, hanging like trapeze ropes from the immense trees, swung out in the wind and fragrant blossoms from the locust tree showered my shoulders and decorated the umbrellalike leaves of the May apple.

I scanned the pathside for a place to take temporary cover just as the huge drops began spattering the waxy leaves here and there. As I neared a small stream my pace was hurried because the raindrops were so cold. I pulled the brim of my hat down to protect my face and made a dash for the old hollow tree where I had spent many a happy childhood hour.

Its base was large enough to get in if I could sit cross-leggedly. The floor was dry with bits of broken pecan shells from the squirrel's storehouse, and long, brown needles from the neighboring pine tree. I had the sensation of warm dry comfort and security as I leaned my head back and watched the raindrops fall like a silver curtain over the opening. It seemed I could sense the tremendous relief of the plants and the leaves of the trees as they vibrated under the constant pattering.

The pace of the shower was spasmodic, with great hard drops halting suddenly, followed by sweeping sheets of mist. Every so often sunlight would break through the clouds and sift through the rainfall like rays of gold. For a moment the sunbeams fell across my lap and touched the palm of my hand like a warm caress. The longer I occupied my niche the more I became a part of the scene. It was so quiet that a rabbit hippety-hopped past my tree, sheltered himself under a pokeberry bush, and nibbled away at a clump of wild lettuce. His long ears were flat against his silky, brown back and his jaws wiggled like gelatin while he feasted.

A loud gru—mp! and a splash of water attracted my attention to the large circle in the creek where a bullfrog had made a belly buster. I watched to see what had frightened him off his wide, flat rock and saw that it was a raccoon waddling along the water's edge. His face had the wisdom and sensitivity of a sage as he fished around the small stones beneath the water. Whatever he found under the rocks to please his persnickety appetite, he washed carefully before carrying it off for his supper.

My rabbit friend suddenly paused in his repast and drew his head down tight and sat motionless. While we listened, soft footsteps drew nearer until two does came into view. To see such beauty at close range is a rare treat any time, but that day their soft brown coats were gleaming wet and satin smooth. They paused on the wet pine needles with the grace of ballet dancers before moving on down to drink. Their limpid, brown eyes were unafraid for they were secure in their forest.

I had learned a childhood lesson that I would never be accepted in the woods until I had learned to blend myself, my thoughts, and my movements to those of the wood-folk. By learning the art of being quiet, by listening and seeing, I am a part of beauty everywhere.

> My misty, mysterious, green-tinted woodland,
> A concert of bird and wind and deer;
> I cannot question your right or wrong,
> For God and love and peace are here!
> Silence

*

When there is no fear of darkness . . . the night is friendly . . . laughter from somewhere . . . cicadas churring in seeming unison . . . moonlight bathing the treetops, and . . . the footsteps of an evening stroller.

Most of the fear we have of darkness . . . is our thought of what might be . . . the same as many fears and unfortunate experiences are generated by thought going in the wrong direction. . . . For we attract to us so much of the wrong by running scared . . . because other people are running scared . . . and in turning our thought to a higher level . . . we find that night is a restful time.

Night throws a cloak of protection and quiet peace about our shoulders . . . allowing us to reflect on the hours before and the hours to come . . . when light will again thrust us into activity . . . and the charm of the night is then impossible. . . . It seems night offers more solitude . . . more opportunity to think more deeply . . . for even great artists and sculptors need long periods of silence and solitude . . . to be

98

creative they must have time to listen and time to vision . . . the constant clamor and interruption of daylight seems to scatter the creative forces.

One of the most important parts of prayer is the need to be quiet and listen . . . to hear an inner wordless voice that speaks through ideas and feelings . . . and ideas cannot come if the din within and around is distracting our attention . . . but night with all its gentleness can quiet disturbed emotions . . . uplift despondent hearts . . . and answer prayers.

*

Amid the clamor and fuss of everyone going in every direction I like to draw up my chair and dream of the quiet things.

There are a lot of beautiful sounds in this world. I love to hear muted sounds from the gentle strings of the violin as well as the distinct sound of a Cadillac horn—but most pleasant and most homelike, I love to hear coffee perking on the stove.

I love to hear children laughing, and I love also the call of a bobwhite very early in the morning or in late evening. I love to hear singing in the kitchen and happy footsteps on the stairs.

But there are some ugly sounds too. Sirens blowing, angry voices, a screaming peacock going to roost. I really don't mind the harsh voice of Petie the peacock, his strut is so beautiful and his attitude so likable. When he fans out his fabulous array of feathers, all gilt tipped and in gorgeous shades of turquoise, he shimmies his soft bloomerlike feathers on his bottom—an act that would put a dancer to shame. When I watch this remarkable bird strut and twirl I have no doubt of a Supreme Being, for how could anything so exquisite be anything but a divine creation.

But I always come back to my peaceful dreams, those thing that quiet my spirit and appease a nature that gets awfull tired sometimes.

Have you ever listened to the silent sounds, a canoe sli ping through the water, a paintbrush against the canvas? Ha you ever heard your bare feet on the sandy beach or listen to the flame on the hearth? Have you noticed the stars si and have you heard the snow fall?

Have you listened to the autumn leaves all shades of ch anthemums drift to the grass, and the early morning mist like vapor in the pine trees? Birds in flight? The so breeze?

Have you ever had life whisper to you that you a part of all that is good? That you can rise above all afflictions, rise above every limitation, lift over the clou sorrow and despair, and bloom as beautifully as any made?

Have you heard your own wordlessness acknowledg deepest appreciation for your every blessing and the being alive in all these quiet things?

If you have a dream to dream of quiet things, e a few brief moments, draw your chair up beside mine ever I have not thought of you will, and it is all th shared.

Chapter 13

"A time to love, and a time to hate. . . ."

If there is something you would so like to do . . . make it
a dream and make it come true. . . . Believe that it will with
all of your heart . . . believe in it fully right from the start.
. . . Feel the success of it, keep it in view . . . make it an
intricate real part of you . . . never let doubt interfere any-
where . . . breathe life into it, think about it and care . . .
what happens, you know, is all up to you. . . . If you love
it enough, your dream will come true!

Chapter 13

"A time to love, and a time to hate . . ."

Every thinking person knows it is easier to love someone and to accept him with a warmer and more natural feeling when this can be spontaneous rather than something expected or demanded.

Making someone feel it is his duty to love, or demanding attention, will surely narrow the chances of anything worthwhile ever developing on its own. So much of the happiness of life is an invitation not a command, a leading and not a pushing.

No one loves us because they ought to, or because our position in life or family demands it, but because we have attracted it to us by our ability to love rightly. Love has been called the bond of perfection and certainly this is the only bond that can endure. For it is every man's urge to be free to express what he chooses to express, and he will be free if only in his thoughts.

We like to think others are the reason we live. It is a wonderful thing to love and be loved. We are inspired by such love to rise above ourselves higher than we thought possible. It gives us reason to rise in the morning, makes us more ready to face the activities of the day, and helps us step more easily over the obstacles. If we become disillusioned about that love, we cannot call it bad.

Love is a channel and if that channel breaks down we cannot be right in falling back to be less than we know we can be. It is then that we should be grateful for the smallest part of that love and know what we have accomplished through it was by and for ourselves. We cannot attach ourselves to another person and make him responsible for us. We are responsible to ourselves, and no one else has the power to make or break us. We merely accept another's love as a gift, but the responsibility is our own.

To receive, one must first give as it has been anonymously written:

Love is the filling from one's own another's cup;
Love is the daily laying down and taking up;
A choosing of the stony path through each new day
That other feet may tread with ease a smoother way.
Love is not blind, but looks abroad through other eyes;
And asks not, "Must I give?" but "May I sacrifice?"
Love hides its grief, that other hearts and lips may sing;
And burdened walks, that other lives may wing.
Hast thou a love like this within thy soul?
'Twill crown the life with blessings when thou dost reach the goal.

*

It was Emerson who said never to lose an opportunity to see something beautiful for beauty is God's handwriting.

We sometimes lose touch with beauty for the mere lack of it in our own hearts. We become so saturated with the grotesque and the unnatural that we allow true beauty to flow away from us until everything becomes dark and unsightly.

Beauty is that quiet something that may be only a feeling,

but it is so right that no one can mistake its source. Beauty can be the scent and sight of orange blossoms in the moist, late evening air, or tender thought and concern for the smallest of life's creatures. It can be the first rays of morning sunlight that lovingly touch the new green leaves of spring, or the brush of human fingers in acknowledgment of something deeper and better than the mundane. Beauty is joy in the laughing face of a child, or soft understanding in a mother's face. Beauty is that which transcends time and space and circumstance, for true beauty is love. And true love is God in action.

*

Hate breaks man away from his power to reason. Every thing worthwhile is forgotten and only a white fury is directed at someone or something.

Hate is an emotion to which the normal person has given little thought. It becomes a word to express a strong dislike, but hate as a strong and passionate dislike is reserved for those persons and those things that are outside the normal person's comprehension. And it is right that he should not waste himself feeling hatred.

If there be anything to hate, it should be the oppression of mankind, the force of ignorance and stupidity, the laxity of standing up for what is right and good, and the imposition of person against person. To stand back and pretend these things do not matter is morally wrong and unforgivable. Most people who cause these things hate themselves first, and could care less what price they have to pay since the main part of them has already been destroyed. To protect them only to allow them the same privilege of imposing their hate again and again on the innocent should in itself be hated. If anyone must give any part of his emotions over to hate, let it be for these things.

*

How could you be anything but good . . . when you have so
instilled in me . . . this freedom, this ability to feel the joy
. . . of just being me without fear and prejudice and lack-
luster.

What are you but the greatest friend . . . who would say
nothing but good to me . . . to lift me past the dark levels I
have known . . . and have given me new vision of both my
inner self and the world about me. . . . What can I say of
you except that I know no greater joy than thinking of you
with love . . . though I may not see you ever again . . . you
have given me so much more than most whom I have always
known . . . so now that life is new and dear . . . shall I not
do as much and pass along to others the right to live and
learn . . . and know that there are such as you?

*

The greatest debt we owe to other people is love. How many
times in the space of a few seconds have others given us the
little something that changed our thinking and changed our
lives.

Suppose the man whistling gala tunes was aware that he
lifted someone's spirits, or that in the darkest mood and fit
of depression someone said something positive and changed
a pattern of wrong thinking to one of success.

Someone's thoughtful consideration makes us feel more
needed and suddenly we too have our places in the world.
And someone asks our help and we know we have something
worthy of giving.

But most of all we owe to God. The cardinals' songs, the
dappled pattern of sunlight on the walk, the delicate petals
of the crocus, and the night song of the merry mimicker.

How great our gifts and even greater our debt of love.

*

Riches consist not in the extent of possessions, but in the ability to appreciate. How great our blessings and how small our appreciation.

The richest people in the world are those who can see the changes of the seasons, the faces of those whom they love and more important, they can see past the doors of prejudice and hate and despair. They are rich because they can breathe deeply the fragrance of flowers, but also peace. They can feel the cool and the heat and the tender touch of a hand, but also the touch of souls.

For these blessed few, food, both spiritual and material, is fully appreciated and enjoyed. Their hearing is tuned to the sounds and songs of the land, but never to sarcasm or cynicism.

The ultimate is love, for to be truly loved is to be truly rich.

Chapter 14

"A time of war, and a time of peace. . . ."

Whether I am walking in the rain . . . or trudging in the snow . . . I know the pressure of your hand . . . to help me as I go . . . along life's path though tired my soul . . . I know I must be true . . . the purpose and the reason for . . . the love I know for you. . . . To lift my chin and steadfast be . . . to keep a clear, dry eye. . . . To know that never in the world . . . would you ever make me cry . . . will keep me prayerfully with you . . . though you be far away. . . . My heart is happy just to know . . . you're coming back one day.

Has there ever been a righteous, just, or holy war? There have been wars that were believed necessary, but can we call them holy?

There are too many impaired personalities involved to call war a thing of spiritual wholeness. The only holiness in any conflict is the unimpaired innocence of those who are involved by requirement or caught in circumstance. The Greek poet Sophocles, over four hundred years before Christ stated wisely: "War loves to seek its victims in the young." And anything that seeks to victimize our young is not worthy of adoration.

If man must fight to feel like a man, he has missed the whole essence and beauty of true manhood, whether it is in the world conflicts, the world of commerce, or in the world of the personal man. The theory of dictatorship, "listen to me and I will create for you a Utopia," has been the bad seed planted in the first mind that started the first war. Sadly, that seed has multiplied and led millions upon millions to go and fight the enemy for reasons they have only been told about, while all about them are the real and terrible enemies —ignorance, disease, superstition, and prejudice.

The wisdom and warm humanity of Winston Churchill was revealed in his expressed thoughts that human tragedy lies in the fact that after all the exertions and sacrifices of millions of people and of the victories for whatever the purpose, righteous cause or peace or security, we still have not found the true meaning of peace and face even greater perils than those we have overcome.

The greatest perils we face lie within man himself. A lasting national stability is dependent entirely upon the individual. Here is where wars begin, with the constant condemnation of leadership, with lack of respect for authority, for family and friends, and secretly for self, until the ultimate is open conflict. When man cannot live with himself, neither can he live with others. His only hope is to change. And resistance to change seems inherent. He is one in armies of people resisting change. Yet, change for the better is the only hope, changes that can take unfamiliar threads from this seeming chaotic contemporary philosophy and weave them into something of lasting value. To love freedom and to love our own does not mean we must hate and make war to keep them. We, who have gone so far past the point of turning back, must instead change our destiny to peace by changing our human patterns.

A time for war? Yes, there is a time for anything we want to strive after. As Greek philosopher Pythagoras wrote, "It is only necessary to make war with five things: with the maladies of the body, the ignorances of the mind, with the passions of the body, with the seditions of the city, and the discords of families." When we overcome these, we shall have overcome the need, or a time, for wars.

*

If I owe no man anything, If I do not step on his toes, infringe on his property, or cause him grief, am I free to do as I please, regardless of what it is?

The philosophy that anyone can live high and handsome

as long as he does not hurt anyone else is ignorant of who "anyone" is. No matter how much he avoids hurting other persons, he forgets that within him is the real self, not the one who puts up fronts, rationalizes the wrongs, and justifies every action, but the one that he trespasses against every time he side-steps justice.

In achieving happiness any man must first be on friendly terms with himself. Nearly eight hundred years ago, Saint Bernard wrote, "Nothing can work me damage except me, and I am the real sufferer by my own fault."

If a man is unhappy with himself, he infringes on the rights of other people by having nothing of himself to contribute to society. He cannot live alone because his house is divided against itself, and a house divided is a house at war.

And yet, how many of us have purchased peace with personal sacrifices. It is said that every time someone does a wrong, someone sacrifices. It seems sometimes the innocent must pay because the guilty will not accept the responsibility. Peace at any price is unreasonable and standing straight with such a burden is impossible. Sooner or later the responsibility must go home to roost and it is the responsibility of the innocent to stand away and allow the guilty room to put down their feet. It is often peace purchased with pain for we do not even leave regret without a little hurt. Can we forget? Forgive perhaps?

Remember the *Rubáiyát* of Omar Khayyam:

> The Moving Finger writes; and, having writ,
> Moves on: nor all your Piety nor Wit
> Shall lure it back to cancel half a line,
> Nor all your tears wash out a word of it.

Perhaps we cannot forget our wars in their entireties, but with forgiveness we can live in peace.

There have always been anxious ages, times when it seemed life could not possibly continue as it was. Since the first record of events there seems to have been more passion than compassion, more giving than receiving, more fear than hope.

There is little use in man's denying his anxiety when it shows so plainly in the way he drives his car, the manner in which he blasts out at other people, blaming them and accusing everyone of being the cause of his trouble.

The fault for all anxiety lies at the center of the one who finds trouble everywhere. This is a fact that mankind does not want to admit, but there are natural laws of attraction and repulsion that he sets into motion by his attitude, whether it is faith-filled or adamant.

Peace must have its beginning place, and it will never be in the midst of fiery anxiety where people are only willing to give what is demanded or whose continual search for wrong seems more important than finding right.

Peace will begin where it is believed possible. It will begin with peaceful persons who believe in good.

To some, peace is nonexistent and life will always be a fight, a continual struggle for a foothold. Hardships and the necessities of life build into such persons a will of iron. They remember too well the times when grit was the only thing that held together body, soul, and spirit. There was born a sort of pride that in the face of impossible odds a fight had taken place and strength of effort, determination, and fortitude had won. Suddenly, the fight itself becomes the important thing, and it represents a trophy testifying that anything less than a struggle is an insult to a fighting spirit.

It is suddenly compulsory that everyone, particularly the young, who know little of the kind of difficulties their elders have experienced, realize how hard and fierce and desperate the fight has been to produce a world of ease for them. And yet in these present days of anxiety, has there been a concentrated effort to give the young the moral and spiritual stamina they need to live with their affluence? They have an even greater need for strength and courage to battle a psychological and emotional war. Perhaps they have been provided only trophies of their elders' physical labors and hardships and a form religion without joy.

Where is the moral and religious link between generation and generation in these times of anxiety? It can be heartbreaking to have tradition tread upon, but even more to those with whom it began. Each generation must have the liberty to follow tradition or to make its own. Whatever son acquires from father cannot be lightly transferred or pushed, but breathed and sensed and loved through with nothing of indebtedness. Dependency and demands create rebellion where "honor thy father and mother" and "provoke not thy children" are overlooked or forgotten. Fulfillment in every generation must come through its own efforts.

There is great consolation in this present day to know that such liberty to seek demands life and cannot be trampled into nothingness. Daniel Webster said it this way, "If the true spark of religious and civil liberty be kindled, it will burn. Human agency cannot extinguish it. Like the earth's central fire, it may be smothered for a time; the ocean may overwhelm it; mountains may press it down; but its inherent and unconquerable force will heave both the ocean and the land, and at some time or another, in some place or another, the volcano will break out and flame to heaven."

There have always been anxious ages, but this one can be less so if generation can say to generation, "What we have done has been for us. It has been our best and has given us reason and purpose and some happiness. We hope it will be for your benefit also, but we only ask that you do what you can, be the best you can in this age, which neither of us yet knows how to handle. Try to make it something with which you can live, something you can reflect to your heirs in hopes it will make their age one of supreme peace."

✳

Most human problems begin because everyone is trying to say the same thing but in a different way. The average person dislikes anything that looks or sounds different from the way he would have expressed it. Can he possibly say anything is less true because it is not said in the way he likes to hear it?

There is an unequaled joy in finding a kindred soul who thinks and believes and acts in a well-known way, but if there were never differences in human beings where would there be growth? Is it not the differences and variety that stimulates deep thinking, self-knowledge, and the desire to stretch the mind?

Strong and beautiful friendships are born because of differences in background and teaching. Basic truths and good and love serve as the foundation for an opportunity to learn even more, and for the excellent opportunity to create a permanent peace.

✳

It is very quiet here among the stars . . . except for their singing I hear only the beat of my own heart . . . and I know from these heights . . . from this level of seeing and feeling . . . how foolish I have been to allow myself to hear anything but the music of the heart and soul . . . for in my lifetime of living on a lower level . . . where one has to take evil into account . . . I heard the voice of the dark and morbid . . . I listened and I contributed to the voice of woe . . . I was bent on telling my own troubles . . . and determined

118

that others should know of my worst conditions . . . that I added to the world's peacelessness and loveless condition . . . and gave off an aura that would attract no more than madness . . . but in rising above those voices I can hear something different . . . and I can look down on my emotions and down on the paths I have been following . . . and I can see how foolish it was to pass my time . . . believing that I could drag to me love in its greatest and most holy sense . . . for no matter what I say, or how beautifully . . . if I have not love . . . I am only talking loudly.

Though I know all the mysteries of life and I am exalted for my knowledge . . . and have not love . . . I am nothing.

If I give everything I have to someone else . . . even if I give my very being to be martyred . . . and I have not love . . . then I am nothing.

I have come to know that love can suffer a long time . . . and it can still be kind and gentle . . . it can only give of itself, never thinking of being envious or resentful . . . for there is sufficient love for every person.

Love is not a proud thing given only to me . . . so that I can point to it as if it were my private accomplishment . . . but it is the highest, the kindest, most gentle, respectful, and giving emotion . . . ever to be experienced . . . it has no need to shout, for its presence is like a garden of flowers I cannot see . . . but their beneficent influence diffuses itself throughout my soul.

I must enjoy again and again the knowledge that love has no need to seek its own . . . that which is mine will come to me . . . in so much greater degree . . . in so much more beauty . . . in so much more holiness than I could ever seek on my own . . . and in the joy of it . . . there is always forgiveness so that regret has no place to gain entrance.

Because love is not continually seeking to find things wrong . . . it is not easily provoked . . . and so it is lasting and forever beautiful . . . no matter where there is great oratory, prophecies, or knowledge . . . they shall all go before this love fails . . .

Here on the heights I am first to catch the sun's rays and last to reflect the rosy glow . . . Now knowing this, how shall I live . . . but with great joy and patience . . . because I am loved, I am something . . . I am grateful!

*

This is the age of questioning. Young and old want to know the reason of things. Why haven't the teachings of the church and our beliefs in a higher power delivered us from war, poverty, and unhappiness in general? What is the meaning of all the rebellion in nearly every phase of life, in areas we thought to be unchangeable? Why is the world running scared, fearfully guarding every minute possession and eyeing every neighbor as a threat?

We were not created alike, we were not expected to respond in the same manner. Regardless of how fallible those who claim to live by faith seem to be, we cannot blame the Creator for the weakness in that response. There must be a willingness to try, a strength and peace within each individual, before there can be peace around the world.

If we cannot get along with the person next to us, how do we expect others to be different? Who are we to blame except ourselves for our inability to shoulder our share of the responsibility? If peace is possible, let it begin with us—as individuals.

Chapter 15

"He hath made every thing beautiful in its
time. . . ."

I shall remember the happy things. I shall remember the special persons, the peaceful, tranquil times. I shall live each moment with some joy, seeing the best in everyone, finding fulfillment in the bird's song, the flowers, the raindrops.

The world responds to me as I say "hello" to it, friendly or cheerless, it is mine to mold second by second.

Regardless of how the past has been, this moment, this day is mine to live. It contains all the ingredients I need to be happy, if only quietly and thoughtfully within myself. That, after all, is part of the reward for thinking, speaking, and remembering only the joys of the past and present.

Since I must walk daily with memories, how much better they be the good ones rather than those best forgotten.

Wrote Henry Ware, American divine, "The shaping of our own life is our own work. It is a thing of beauty, or a thing of shame, as we ourselves make it."

✳

There seems to be a time for every thing . . . a creative time when we begin to build something new . . . a time of order when we put every thing in its right place . . . a time of sadness when laughing is at one end and crying at the other . . .

playing Yo-yo with the emotions. . . . There is a time when the pendulum of faith swings very high and in its full swing also finds the lows . . . there is a time when amiability and agreement are light and easy . . . and a time when there is no neutral ground on which to work . . . a time for sheer happiness so that nothing is accomplished except on dancing feet . . . and a time when the spirit is so submerged in the God everywhere present, that a lack of courage would be impossible.

Life has so much more beauty than unpleasantness that we cannot ignore the comet's tail . . . the meteor flashing across a star-studded sky . . . a cool breeze carrying the fragrance of honeysuckle . . . the early dawn misty pink and golden . . . a sweet sleep full of quiet breathing and happy dreams . . . the sun's golden tanning . . . the salt air's tangy breath . . . and every man's faith that takes him nearer his God and love.

We cannot forget the opportunity, the time of challenge . . . the moment of truth, the discovery of a new self we have not known . . . the fear that can melt away with a little courage . . . the aching with love for the hurt of someone else . . . the miracle of a baby . . . a rippling brook, the singing trees. . . . There is a purpose to every thing under heaven . . . for He has made every thing beautiful in its time.

*

"A thing of beauty is a joy forever; its loveliness increases; it will never pass into nothingness; but still will keep a bower quiet for us, and a sleep full of sweet dreams, and health, and quiet breathing." These beautiful words are from John Keats's *Endymion.* The healing power of peaceful rest.

If only in these nervous times we could go to that place of beauty. If only we could put down every responsibility and turn for a few moments to the loveliness that increases.

What is beauty? Is it grace? Charm? Fair of face? Or is it something even better, something unseen but felt? Perhaps it is the soul of man.

Beauty is that which everyone expects to find in tangible things and only finds the search to be endless. In its true essence it is all that we love and hold sacred, the true meaning behind all meanings, the love behind all loves, and the deep spiritual mystique hidden in man where he seldom thinks to look for it. It is that which makes everything beautiful in its time.

*

The sky is a woman, changeable and ever-changing. She can wear the smooth, sun-washed face of gentle smiles and suddenly lift her black brows in a stormy rage, split the heavily charged atmosphere with sharp tongues of lightning, and loose torrents of tears without regard for the innocent. But for her changeable ways she possesses the profound and basic constancy that has guided man by her stars, warmed him with sunlight, refreshed him with raindrops, and romanced him with moonlight. Her personality varies with the season, the day, the hour, and the moment to correspond with her most extraordinary display of colorful gowns and dazzling array of jewels. No man has ever learned the depths of her infinite soul and no man has been allowed to follow all the secret channels of her heart. They can only study and surmise, probe and make guesses that later may be proved wrong. Her airways support the great wings of the golden eagle and the gigantic superjets in their long flights. Space capsules orbit the earth through her vacuum but no one possesses her and no one questions her position.

Morning so often finds her still half asleep, still adorned with her jewels from the night before. Then she comes forth quickly in her blue morning coat and rose-tinted cheeks to touch the earth with dew-laden kisses and to rejoice with a chorus of bird song. Man loses when he sleeps past this magic hour, when he could let his spirit soar to touch the first rays of the morning sun, for it is in the freeing of his spirit that he is eventually free in all other ways. Not anything physical or material can bind him when his spirit flies straight up to those infinite, fathomless depths.

The midday sun washes the sky to palest blue so that even the wings of the highflying gull, once tinted the green of the sea, are lost from vision. It is impossible to face such brilliance with the naked eye, but the sun's influence is felt everywhere. Life-giving rays tan and heal man's body. The seeds he plants are sprouted and drawn through the earth's crust to productivity. As the earth makes its annual revolution around the sun, all the varying degrees of heat and cold are felt in her ethereal atmosphere. There was no human to witness this beginning, but the Creator is the Master Artist making a journey through space too marvelous to comprehend.

The evening sky, like embers upon the hearth, sets strange shadows across the land. Tints of amethyst and sapphire are tinged with gold and streaked with the deep red of the rainbow. Swift flights of birds and wandering thistledown are silhouetted for a brief moment. And suddenly there is nothing left of the day but the faint rose-colored fabric of content. The day is done. It is twilight time. Like early morning it is a delightful mixture of night and day, except in reverse. Instead of the bright bird voices, now they murmur and cheep in their good-night ceremonies. And there is one still too full of joy to contain it all. He sings out, sounding as out of place in the quiet as laughing aloud in the chapel.

Overhead the evening star boldly adorns the breast of the sky, and one by one the fabulous curve of her cheek gathers the fiery stones. In a mood of frivolity she flings them across the heavens, leaving flames and vapor trailing behind. The round, jolly face of the moon moves up in the eastern sky, silvering the edges of a stray white cloud and paling the stars with the exception of the brightest. Their bewitchment and beauty have inspired poets from Homer and the author of Job down to Tennyson. Men of fancy have compared them to fireflies, dewdrops, and diamonds.

There is so much mystery and beauty in our Lady's unfathomable depths. The first simple shepherds tending their flocks in the meadows named the stars that guided them. One perfect star, splendid in its brilliance and purpose, led Wise Men to a new beginning.

This cerulean lady is an ever-changing Masterpiece. She, indeed, is a timeless beauty.

＊

Come with me through the snow-filled woods and feel their quiet peacefulness reach into your very soul. Here in the serenity of this trackless forest there is communion with life in its deepest sense. There is a contrast between the bright flash of the redbird's wings and the soft furry blending of cottontails with the snow. An even greater contrast lies between the quiet air where breath hangs in a misty vapor and the moving, thriving life beneath the blanket of white where nature is already preparing for another season.

Above our heads the trees interlock their ice-covered branches forming a gossamer pattern as intricate as the spider's web. The air is so crystal clear that the tinkling of a cowbell carries across from the woodland barnyard. The skaters on the pond and the sleds along the slope have rhythm and movement in keeping with the long, silent strains of sound heard, but unheard. To stand breathlessly, still relates to the timelessness, the seeming weightlessness of a thousand diamonds caught in space.

Is this forever? There are no visible signs of change. There is nothing to promise that these woods will ever give birth to new life. Truly every thing is beautiful in its time, but every thing must continuously have a new season in which to be beautiful, a breaking up to rebuild. Even in the beauty and healing solitude of these beautiful woods, we must know that this too shall pass. It will pass in the orderly procession of nature that it might come again, not as a cold, barren waste, but as a magical mystical winter wonderland that breathes silently and majestically with pulsating life and purpose.

＊

To every thing a season, a purpose for every thing under heaven. All of life has a reason. Each part of our lives has a purpose. A time of birth, a time of growth, a time of maturity, a time of death. In between each purposeful and significant division, lies all the hurts, all the tears, all the smiles, all loves that make us the persons we are. Even regrets have a purpose, if only to realize how good it is to have raised our sights again.

The poetry and simplicity of the Indian's life is so expressed;

A time to sing
A time to sigh
A time to laugh
A time to cry
A time to live
A time to die

A time to let go the old so that newness of mind and spirit can come in. For He has made every thing beautiful in whatever stage it is in.